Jacquie – [handwritten inscription] of His life as you grow stronger every day!

The
Presence Powered
Life

Supernatural Living
for the Common Man

[handwritten signature]

REV. CARL B. JENKS

V.I.P.
Vision Imprints Publishing, Inc.
A Thomas Nelson Company
Tulsa, Oklahoma

Endorsements

It is a rare and wonderful thing to call a book "cutting-edge." However, Apostle Carl Jenks has given the Church just that...a truly cutting edge work. It is both inspirational and revelational.

Denny Cramer
Dennis Cramer Ministries

I have known Carl as a friend for over fifteen years. To some extent, I have walked beside him as he has sought to penetrate the depths of the reality of Christ's power and presence within. It has been a costly journey for Carl, but one that has brought the reward of insight to enrich us all. In this book, Carl presents the presence and power of Christ's life in us, first providing inner peace and joy, then overflowing in grace empowering us say and do the Father's bidding. Carl is living the implications of this message. I commend his work to you.

Dan Davis
Pastors in Covenant
Austin, Texas

I have closely walked with Carl Jenks in Christian ministry now for over fifteen years. The crucially powerful and foundational message of "The Presence Powered Life" comes from a rich walk with God that has endured deep testing and produced mature fruit. I was much enriched by reading it.

George Miley
International Director
Antioch Network

Destined to minister hope on the Christian life, Apostle Carl Jenks, through the powerful messages he has revealed from the book of Colossians 1:27, has touched and transformed many lives. My wife Beth and I personally have seen the glory of Jesus Christ being a great hope in our lives. Apostle Carl not only preaches or teaches but he also lives the same life full of the glory of our Lord Jesus Christ. I predict this anointed message continue transforming and setting millions of people free to live the lives God intended.

Bishop Jeremiah and Pastor Beth Pallangyo
Founders,
New Hope for All Nations Church
Naivasha, Kenya

In an elegant and straightforward way Carl Jenks chronicles his journey into a deeper and more joyful relationship with God. In the style of Christian disciplers throughout the millennia Carl will draw his readers along with him into this deeper relationship. Truly this is an important book for the beginning of this new century!

Fr. Robert A. Dalgleish
Founding Pastor
Trinity Communion Church (CEC)
Rochester, New York

THE PRESENCE POWERED LIFE
© 2006 by Carl B. Jenks

Published by Insight Publishing Group
8801 S. Yale, Suite 410
Tulsa, OK 74137
918-493-1718

ISBN: 1-599510-02-2
Library of Congress catalog card number:2005935890

Printed in the United States of America

Dedication

To: the Lord Jesus Christ, "the Way the Truth, and the Life." He is the revealer of all that follows. He has totally transformed me by His might through the "Presence Powered Life."

Contents

Preface

Have you ever been on a very exciting, and at times down right scary car ride? Perhaps it was over mountains and along the edges of steep cliffs. You come winding around a bend and whoa! You are suddenly confronted with an incredible drop off on *your* side of the car and what appears to be a-way-too-steep-climb ahead of you. At times you aren't even sure what your final destination is. "How will I know that I have arrived?", you wonder.

This is the apt description of a journey I have been on for the last several years with the "family" at New Hope Community Church in Rochester, NY. It began with what we thought was a "nice" devotional study of God's love for us. While we have been enriched through the original study, God has taken us to heights and depths we never expected. Along the way we were challenged to leave our comfort zones and "get out of the boat" like Peter. What we have discovered is that God's love is more full of adventure than we ever thought!

The Presence Powered Life is a chronicle of that amazing journey and the wonderful, transforming Life He has revealed to us. I invite you to buckle up, and hold on tight, as we set out. Along the way the Holy Spirit will ask you, as He has us, to release old ways of thinking that have shaped our lives and spirituality. You may think you need them, but in reality, excess baggage is a hindrance to the supernatural life He has for each and every one of us. Ready? Believe me, it is worth the ride!

Acknowledgements

I want to thank:

My wonderful editor, chief inspiration, and life companion. Without the encouragement of my lovely wife Susi this work would not see the light of day. Thank you, my love.

My children, Stephen and Rachel, willing sounding boards in the early days of the working out of this revelation, and constant sources of encouragement. Best of all, they are now walking in the Power themselves.

Ralph Van Auken, Mark DeCory, Glenn Fadner, Rex Fisher and Paul Daniels, the elders and my faithful fellow laborers at New Hope Community Church. Thank you guys for believing in me enough to let this journey take place. It has been quite a ride.

The amazing church family at New Hope Community Church. It has been an honor to walk this path together with each and everyone of you. Your words of encouragement, support and prayers mean more than you will ever know.

Special thanks to David Seaman for his eleventh hour technical expertise.

Bishop Jeremiah and Pastor Beth Pallangyo, of New Hope for All Nations Church in Naivasha, Kenya, and Apostle Edward Steven Kabunga of Christian Living Water Church in Kampala, Uganda for opening themselves and their churches to me to teach this truth. The results have been more than we could have imagined!

Finally you the reader: Thank you for taking the time to read and digest what follows. My prayer for you is that the truth in this little book will become as explosive in your life as it has in mine.

Introduction

We who are disciples of Jesus Christ are on a journey with the Lord. This book is about one man's journey, mine, yet it is also about all of our journeys. I say that, because I believe the revelation that the Lord has given me is for the whole Body of Christ. My experience in some ways, has been unique. Each one of us is unique and special to our Heavenly Father. He doesn't deal with us as statistics, numbers devoid of personality. He loves us all and treats us individually as "the apple of His eye". Yet when one of us receives something from His heart, it is meant to enrich the whole of His family. Such is my story, and the reason for this book. I believe I have received something from Father, a love gift of revelation from Father that He wants to benefit all.

The Lord Jesus came to earth in human form, the Son of Man and the Son of God. He came to fulfill the will of His Father. Man was separated from the fellowship and purposes of God. We had proved in an over 4000 year history that we as a race and as individuals were incapable of living a life pleasing to God. Sinners all, we stood justly condemned under God's righteous judgement. We were deserving of only His wrath. Jesus came to live a sinless life in the flesh, and to die as the sinless Lamb of God in our stead. "He who knew no sin became sin on our behalf, so that we might become the righteousness of God in Him."[1] Praise God for His Matchless Gift!

But, have you ever wondered if there were reasons that Jesus took on human flesh in addition to His coming as the Lamb of God? Dying on the cross and rising again from the grave He made a way for us to be restored to His Father's purposes. But was there anything else? I believe that the answer to that question is a resounding, "Yes!"

Jesus came to show us the Father. "He who has seen me has seen Me has seen the Father..."[2] Why was this important? First, because of dead religion and tradition no one or few at that time had any idea what God the Father was actually like. Because sin had separated them from Him, they could not get close enough to see for themselves. Jesus was the living embodiment of the Father.[3] The Father was through Jesus introducing people who were to come into His family through the cross, to the real person of Who they would be united with in the Kingdom that would become theirs' through the resurrection.

Jesus also came to show us how to live in the new Kingdom. He did this by doing just three things. He only did what He saw the Father doing.[4] He only said what He heard the Father saying.[5] And He only went where the Father told Him to go. How was this possible? He was living by the Life of Another! Jesus was yielded to the life of His Father, Who indwelt Him.[6] By living in total dependence upon the Life of His Father, Jesus was showing us the way we are to live in His Kingdom, in total dependence upon His life in us. Does that sound farfetched, possible, even Biblical? Hold on to your hats and come along with me as we explore together "The Presence Powered Life"

---

1. 2 Corinthians 5:21
2. John 14:9
3. Colossians 2:9
4. John 5:19
5. John 5:30
6. John 14:10-11

Chapter One

Confessions of a "Practical Atheist"

A s a young 20-something I gave my heart to Jesus Christ and became a "born again Christian". Others would call it "being redeemed" or saved. I was water baptized according to the command of the Lord and have experienced the reality of the Holy Spirit in my life. The fellowship of believers in small groups and large gatherings, regular attendance of church services, prayer and Bible study has been my practice. I have read the Bible from Genesis to Revelation over thirty times and practice biblical meditation as a personal discipline. My two grown children have heard worship and Bible verses in our home since infancy, and my wife and I endeavored to "train up a child in the way he should go".[1] Lastly, I left a lucrative career in advertising to become a pastor at the Lord's call and have preached, prayed, counseled and traveled to other nations in His service.

By now it probably sounds like I am tooting my own spiritual horn. But in reality, I am about to share with you a startling discovery. You see, despite genuine fervency and most sincere efforts to be a Christian, I discovered that I was actually living my life as a "Practical atheist". Now that doesn't mean I was *practically* an atheist. No, it is much more subtle than that.

"Whoa, boy", you say, "That's a pretty strong statement for someone who has been a believer in Jesus for as long as you to assert. And, from a pastor no less!"

I understand what you are saying. In fact, I would have said the same things myself a couple of years ago. But the Lord has recently opened my eyes to truths I have read for years, even preached on, but never really "saw". It is amazing how we can read the scriptures over and over but never see the most obvious truth until *He* opens the eyes of our understanding, as He did for the disciples on the road to Emmaus. Like theirs, my heart was burning while He has been explaining the Scripture to me.[2]I believe that its good news that He wants me to communicate to others as well. That is why I am writing this. His message is burning in my bones; I must get it out.

"Lord Jesus, Lover of my soul and He who inhabits my innermost being, please speak through me all that You desire. As *You* did when You were on earth in the flesh, allow me to 'speak only that which I hear from the Father.' I yield myself to You and ask that both the reader and I will understand what You want to say to us now. Grant us a 'Spirit of wisdom and revelation' in the knowledge of You. In Your Name, Amen."

That last petition is a good place to begin our journey. You see, I have come to understand that knowledge is what "tripped me up". Now, I don't mean that knowledge is a bad thing. On the contrary, it is essential. One of my greatest longings is that God's people would be filled with knowledge of the scriptures, i.e. Biblically literate. The problem is not *knowledge*, but *how* we get it. The portion of the verse quoted in my prayer is taken from Ephesians chapter one.[3] It gives us the key to *how* we should be receiving our knowledge. What we need is a "Spirit of wisdom and revelation". If we want to know God and Jesus Christ His Son, really know Him, there is no other way. It takes God to reveal God to man. I would describe that what has happened to me as exactly that. In response to Paul's Holy Spirit inspired prayer, the Lord has granted me such a spirit of revelation and has turned my world *right side* up, theologically, and every other way. In the process, He has also turned my previously attained *"knowledge"* upside down. Hang on and I will explain.

First of all, let's look at the term "practical atheist". Simply put, it is confessing one truth with your mouth and yet living by a different "truth" altogether. By this I do not mean "hypocrisy". A "hypocrite", as I understand it, is one who says one thing and deliberately does another. "Practical atheism", a term the Lord gave me, is the subconscious belief system that comes out in our actual choices and behaviors. Perhaps another way to phrase it is the contrast between our *theoretical beliefs* (what we say we believe) and our *operating beliefs* (how we actually live). We often think that we believe some one or something, but our behavior reveals an entirely different picture.

For me, the issue is distilled to the following questions: "Where is Jesus Christ now? How should that affect my daily life?" There are several answers to these questions. Yes, Jesus ascended to the Father's right hand.[4] He is in heavenly places interceding for us.[5] He is waiting for His enemies to be made His footstool.[6] He is ruling and reigning and holding all things together by the word of His power.[7] These are just a few correct statements. However, the strategic question for me is, "Where is Jesus in relationship to me?" The Bible tells me that when I got saved Jesus came *into* me—into my heart. Even children tell us that. For example, when my son, Stephen, prayed to receive Christ at 2½ years of age, my wife asked him "Where is Jesus now?" His reply was, to point to his chest with a smile and say, "In my heart". I myself have used this terminology for decades at the altar, in counseling and preaching, and in my own confession. However, I have come to understand that, for all those years, it was merely a *theoretical*, not an *operational* belief in my life.

This began to change about three years ago when I embarked on writing a study guide/devotional for my church family to begin the new year; I entitled it *Extravagant Love*.[8] I had no idea just *how* extravagant His love was nor the lengths to which He has gone to enable me to live in His love, that is until He began to show me first hand. Most Christians will readily acknowledge that He loved me (and you) so much, that He died on the cross to remove every hindrance to our being able to know His love. But even more amazing than His sacrifice is that for everyone who receives this gift of eternal life, He, Jesus, has actually, literally, taken up residence in each and every believer so that we might now live on this planet in and by the power of His life and love.

I had unknowingly been carrying a weight I was never meant to carry. Though I was sincerely confessing that Christ was within me, I was living my life as though He weren't, as though Jesus was still somehow on the "outside". The result was that I continually prayed and tried to get closer to Him. How can you get "closer" to someone Who is already living on the inside?! For me it was very frustrating! Jesus is saying, "I am right here." But I was asking, "Lord, where are You? How can I get close to You?" I tried all kinds of things in an attempt to get some where I already was! Now mind you, they were *good things*, but they were *my* efforts to accomplish what I could never achieve, and what has already been done *for* me! The end result of my struggling is that I rarely felt close to the Lord; yet He is the One who inhabits the very core of my being!

So, what did this "practical atheism" look like? Jesus said, "I am the vine, you are the branches; he who abides in Me and I in him, he bears much fruit, for apart from Me you can do nothing."[9] Practical atheism operates in contrast with this vine-branch relationship in the following ways:

☐ I *confess* that Jesus is in me, according to the Scriptures, but I *live* my daily life as though He is not in residence there. Everything depends on my strength, wisdom, ingenuity, etc., not His.

This one has been true in my life in three ways. I have chosen to title them, Good Days, Not so Good Days, and Bad days.

1. Good Days: I have my daily "quiet time" with the Lord. I tell Him how much I love Him and need Him. I receive something from His word or an impartation from Him into my spirit. It

is a wonderful sweet time. One just like the devotional books say should be my daily experience. Then, I go about my daily routine, responding with my own reasoning and "strengths", totally forgetting to be continually dependent on Him for everything, even as I had so tenderly confessed I would be at the start of the day. At bedtime I remember Him again as I close the day with prayer. I thank Him for making it through and for all that He did on my behalf that I was *unaware* of. What joy and fellowship have I missed with Jesus because I was not consciously aware of His abiding Presence throughout the day? In the Sixteenth Century lived a monk named Brother Lawrence; he understood the secret joy and power in God-aware-living. Whatever he did, whether at prayers, working in the garden, or buying supplies for the abbey, Bro. Lawrence carried on a continual conversation with the Lord. Not just speaking *to* Him but listening to Him speak as well! He often said that he was as much at home with the Lord in his daily routine, as he was in private prayer. A wonderful little book has been compiled of his simple, profound lifestyle entitled, *The Practice of His Presence.*[10] The "Spirit of wisdom and revelation" manifest in a former generation, still speaking to God's people...

2. The Not so Good Days: We all have these I am sure. Days that come upon us with so much to do that we do not have time/make the time to spend with the Lord before activity overtakes us. The result is that I go through the day

with an uneasy feeling of being separated from the Lord and His power. Because I have not come to Him in the "right time" or the "right way" I don't feel free to ask for His help as I might on a "Good Day". I am acting in ignorance of the truth that He is always with me. He is in me and desires to live His life through me in the practical issues of life. Perhaps one of the most freeing revelations I have had on this journey is that Jesus is always ready to manifest His life in mine. It does not depend on me or my daily "piety".

3. Bad Days: These are the days when trials or temptations are particularly strong. On these kind of days I often end up sin or "storm" focused rather than Christ focused. The temptation or trial looms large, at times much larger than my faith, especially if I am relying on my own strength, but don't seem to have much! You see, I was never meant to live life apart from Jesus. He really meant it when He said, "Apart from Me you can do nothing."[11] He alone has the power to overcome sin and trial. That power is always readily available to you and me because He is in us.

❐ As a practical atheist I say that He is *in* me and I live through Him, yet I only depend on Him for "spiritual" aspects of my life.

This one is much more prevalent in the church than we realize. We have no problem looking to the Lord for inspiration in songs, worship, prayer, the prophetic, etc. in the service on Sunday or cell group. Yet, we neglect to have the same expectation when it comes to our jobs, our homes, or our studies, just to name a few. Jesus has shown me that He desires to be involved in every aspect of my life. Where I go the King goes. And where the King goes He intends to manifest His Kingdom...everywhere...every day.

Here are a few of the ramifications of this "spiritual schizophrenia", which we will cover in later chapters.

- Even though I am saved, I continually act as though the cross still stands between Him and me.
- I am sin conscious, not Christ conscious
- I am denying the power of the gospel
- I rob myself of the power of the resurrected Christ for *every* aspect of my life.
- I walk in a measure of Spiritual blindness and shortsightedness.
- I constantly battle a sense of defeat instead of victory, condemnation instead of confidence
- I postpone my enjoyment of God's eternal purpose and plan to "by and by in heaven".
- I end up embracing a form of godliness and deny its power.[12]
- The world does not see Him in me!

What I have come to understand is that this is a question of mind vs. revelation. We think we know something, because we have a mental understanding, or think we do. In reality we haven't got a clue! There is a huge difference between mental "knowing" and heart "knowing"—revelation knowledge. Praise God! He is bringing further revelation knowledge in our day. This is an issue of restoring truth to the church. As Dr. Bill Hamon would put it,

"Present Truth" is being restored to the church to enable her to accomplish the purposes of Christ for this generation. It's not that the church has been walking in error; it's just that the Lord is opening our spiritual eyes to truths that have been there all along, but have been hidden until now. He is revealing more of His mysteries, "secrets" He has kept for this generation of Saints to know and walk in. And we get to be a part!

1. Proverbs 22:6
2. Luke 24:32
3. Ephesians 1:17
4. Mark 16:19, Ephesians 1:20
5. Romans 8:34, Hebrews 7:25
6. Hebrews 10:13
7. Hebrews 1:3
8. Extravagant Love, A 30-Day interactive devotional by the author. Available through New Hope Community Church, www.newhopecom.org
9. John 15:5
10. The Practice of His Presence, Brother Lawrence, Whitaker House Publishers 1982
11. John 15:5b
12. 2 Timothy 3:5

Study Questions

"Confessions of a Practical Atheist"

1. Did the author's chapter title and "confession" surprise you? Were there points that you could identify with from your own spiritual journey?

2. Jesus said in Matthew 15:18-19 that out of the fullness of the heart we speak and act. How is it possible to believe one thing with your mind and have something else come out of your heart and mouth?

3. How would you answer the following questions:

   ▪ Where is Jesus Christ now?

   ▪ How should that affect my daily life?

Chapter Two

"Let's start at the very beginning...

A very good place to start..." As the famous song goes.[1]

"In the beginning God..."[2] Everything starts and ends in Him and with Him.[3]

In the beginning God created man. Why? We need to see man's creation from two perspectives in order to understand it.

God's perspective: God created man for fellowship and communion. The Father, Son and Holy Spirit had always enjoyed perfect fellowship and unity. God's desire was to create man to share in that blessed and blissful reality. He was looking for a creature upon whom He could lavish His love, someone to rule and reign with Him on earth and throughout eternity; someone who could bear His image and contain His life. Ultimately, all things, including, and perhaps especially man, were created for His good pleasure.[4]

Man's perspective: The Westminster Catechism asks the question: "What is the chief and highest end of man?" The answer: "Man's chief and highest end is to glorify God and to fully enjoy Him forever."[5] That is the desire placed in every human heart by our Creator and Father. Man's greatest pleasure comes when he is fully engaged in fellowship and communion with His Creator. God's highest pleasure is that man would find his delight in being His.

There must have been incredible exuberance in God's heart when He created man. This was His last and highest level of earthly creation—"Very Good!" He exclaimed. His pride and joy. Man would be the one, the only one, in all of creation with whom He would share dominion. Man was the only one who could receive and return His love. Man was the only one created in God's image. Man was the only one with whom God would walk. Oh, He walked among the other creatures in the Garden, but He walked deliberately *with* man. Lastly, man was the only one in all this creation with freedom of choice and will. He alone could chose to return or spurn God's love; to obey or disobey Him.

God's highest creation was also His greatest "gamble". Though in His Omniscience, He knew man would fall, He proceeded to create him anyway. Why take the risk? You see, the greatness of God's love requires someone who can love Him *freely*. Love without the risk of not being loved in return, is not love at all. Love without choice is not love. When He did this, Father was not being driven by an emotional need to be loved. God needs nothing. He is completely complete in Himself. The Father, Son and Holy Spirit have enjoyed perfect love from eternity past. The creation of man is the expression of the largeness of His heart, a love that stops at nothing to find a suitable object of expression. This love cannot be contained, but must continually be shed abroad, deposited in more and more hearts.[6] It has been said that since God uttered the words, "Let there be light", light has been going ever outward. In the last few years even scientists have begun to come around to this way of thinking, acknowledging that the universe is continually expanding! The same is true of His love. It is ever moving outwards, encompassing more and more loved ones.

And so God began with one—Adam. We don't know how long it was just Adam and God. It must have been for some time, because it certainly took awhile for Adam to name all the animals and to discover that in all that number there was not a helpmate suitable for him.[7] Certainly God and Adam walked together for a season before God decided it was time to add to His family. In His great love for Adam, He created Eve, even though He knew that with each additional person His "gamble" increased. But that did not matter to Him, because His love is always bigger than any risk to Himself.

Adam and Eve walked with God in the cool of the day—"Man's chief and highest end"! It was the fullness of joy for Father and children. But there was another figure in the shadows...

Satan hates it when man enjoys what he (Satan) lost, and more![8]

Then came the fall. "Loves labors lost"?

The promise of restoration.[9]

Was this a new beginning? Or was it merely a momentary detour for the creature, not the Creator?

What was God's ultimate intention?

What if "the fall" was only a momentary detour for man and not God? Have you ever stopped to think about that? We tend to presume, and have indeed been taught, that the fall created this un-crossable chasm between the Father and us. The rest of His plan was to try and fix it by seeing that chasm bridged. Therefore, the ultimate act of God was sending His Son to die to pay the debt for our sin. Christ, The Bridge, spanned the chasm. This certainly is wonderful news for the whole human race. But I am left wondering why did the Lord do it that way? Why didn't He just wipe man out and start again? He said to Moses that He could do that if He chose to.[10] Instead, the Bible traces the account differently. Father began again and again and again with the man He had already created, and moved from individuals, to a family, to a people.

What was His ultimate intention? Was it the salvation of the individual from sin, or was it something more? I believe that it was something much, much more. Yes, sin was an obstacle to be overcome, but only because it hindered man from continuing in God's eternal plan. God has always desired and sought for a people in whom He could *dwell*. He began with individuals, then a family, then a people, but His ultimate objective was to create a body for One! Sin in man delayed that, but only for a while. His plan has always been for a many-membered body in which to dwell. No longer is it "Emmanuel" God with us, relating from the outside. But, "Emmanuel" God within! And He had it in mind all along. His intention, His search has been for a people for His own possession. "But you are a chosen race, a royal priesthood, a holy nation, a people for God's own possession..."[11]

The revelation of this mystery[12] transformed my life and is the reason and the subject of this book.

1 The Sound of Music, Rogers & Hammerstein
2. Genesis 1:1
3. Romans 11:36
4. Revelation 4:11 (KJV)
5. Westminster Shorter Catechism, Question 1
6. Romans 8:5
7. Genesis 2:20
8. Revelation 12:7-17
9. Genesis 3:15,21
10. Exodus 32:10
11. 1 Peter 2:9
12. Colossians 1:27

Study Questions

"Let's Start at the Very Beginning"

1. Our God is a loving Father and Creator, not an impersonal "force", as some have labeled Him. Have you ever considered why He was moved to create YOU? Spend time today considering this. Then write a sentence in your own words about the "why" of Creation—both from God's perspective and your own. If you are studying this book with a group, share your answers with each other.

2. How do you respond to the idea that the Fall was only a "temporary detour" for man in God's plan?

Chapter Three

A Tale of Two Trees

"The Lord God planted a garden toward the east, in Eden; and there He placed the man whom He had formed. Out of the ground the Lord God caused to grow every tree that is pleasing to the sight and good for food; the tree of life also in the midst of the garden, and the tree of the knowledge of good and evil."[1]

Have you ever wondered why there were two trees in the midst of the Garden? Of one tree, the tree of the knowledge of good and evil, we are unfortunately, all too well aware. But what about the other one? You know, the tree of life?

How did the tree of life figure into His eternal plan? We get an idea by reading what the Lord did after the fall to keep Adam and Eve away from it.

"Then the Lord God said, 'Behold, the man has become like one of Us, knowing good and evil; and now, he might stretch out his hand, and take also from the tree of life, and eat and live forever'— therefore the Lord God sent him out from the garden of Eden..."[2]

If the tree of the knowledge of good and evil made man like God, how much more would the tree of life! My sense is, that God intended all along for man to eat of the latter, but the former needed to be there also because of free will. Man was given the choice to eat and the choice to obey or not, with the consequences clearly delineated. God's expulsion of them from the garden was necessary once the fruit of the tree of the knowledge of good and evil had been tasted, to prevent a premature eating of that tree of life. But what do you suppose would have happened if Adam and Eve had eaten of the tree of life first? Does the Lord give us some clues?

Let's start by examining the trees themselves. Both were in the "midst of the garden", signaling that both were central to God's plan. What else?

Two trees in the garden... I wonder what they were like. We know from Scripture that Eve was fascinated with the tree of the knowledge of good and evil. "...The tree was good for food...a delight to the eyes...and...was desirable to make one wise."[3]

How about the tree of life? What was it like? Our imagination might picture something even more spectacular. After all, it was the *tree of life*. But for Eve and Adam, it certainly didn't hold any special attraction when compared to the tree of knowledge of good and evil. Perhaps the tree of life was not much to look at. Maybe it was just "ordinary", or even marred. It reminds me of another 'tree', the shoot of the stem of Jesse. "He grew up before Him like a tender shoot, and like a root out of parched ground; He has no stately form or majesty that we should look upon him, nor appearance that we should be attracted to Him."[4]

If only Adam and Eve had feasted on <u>that</u> tree! I have heard it postulated that the tree of life was a "prophetic sign" pointing to the eternal life that was to come with redemption. Personally, I struggle with that idea. I believe God had much more in mind. Is it possible that the "tree of life" was a manifestation of the One Who declares Himself to be "the Life"? Was *He*—Jesus, actually the tree of life in the garden? If it was indeed so and they had eaten, would the *incarnation*, God in man, have taken place right then, without the necessity of the cross?

In my journey I have come to believe that the Lord always desired to live in His people. The incarnation of the Son in a body of human flesh was not merely part of the plan of redemption. The incarnation of the Son into the very beings of God's entire family has always been the plan of the Father from the beginning; and I believe, could have happened in the Garden of Eden.

So, what was Jesus' purpose in coming to earth?

1.Genesis 2:8-9
2.Genesis 3:22-3
3.Genesis 3:6
4.Isaiah 53:2-3

Study Questions

"A Tale of Two Trees"

1. Why do you think there were two trees in the Garden?

2. What are your thoughts regarding the author's hypothesis on the identity of the Tree of Life?

Chapter Four

The Mystery

" *T* *o whom God willed to make known what is the riches of the glory of this mystery among the Gentiles, which is Christ in you the hope of glory."*[1]
In Greek it is the word *muste⁻rion* (moos-tay'-ree-on): "From a derivative of muo⁻ (to *shut* the mouth); a *secret* or "mystery" (through the idea of *silence* imposed by *initiation* into religious rites):— mystery."[2]

So, what is the mystery?

Man was never created to live apart from union with God. All of what we in the church refer to as "redemptive history" points to that fact. In the Old Testament account, even with the very Law of God, the Ark and the Presence in their midst His people Israel were not able to live a life pleasing to Him. Man could not stay the course on his own. Someone had to come, to make the way for us back into God's plan for the ages, and to show us how to live as God had always planned for us to live. Jesus did both.

We are familiar in our theology with His making a way for us. Through His sinless life and death on the cross as payment for our sins, the Lord Jesus redeemed us from the curse of sin that we had

come under when our first parents ate of the
forbidden fruit. Our debt was paid and fellowship
with the Father restored. Once again we stood in the
place where we could be the habitation of the Most
High. Could this be one of the reasons, if not the
chief reason, why the Holy Spirit says in the book of
Hebrews, "For the joy set before Him He endured
the cross despising its shame."[3] Was the "joy set
before Him", seeing the restoration of the human
creation back to the Godhead's original plan?

It is in the "showing" aspect of the life of Jesus
that we gain further insight into this truth. Jesus
did not come just to redeem mankind from the fall.
The life of the man Jesus was to be a demonstration,
a pattern for redeemed man to follow. Jesus demonstrated how to live in this earthly realm as a habitation of the Lord God Himself.

Consider Jesus' words in, "The Son can do
nothing of Himself unless, it is something He sees
the Father doing; for whatever the Father does,
these things the Son also does in like manner."[4]
Jesus' words have become for me a wonderful
promise and a great challenge. I have come to understand and believe that they are written for our
instruction. We, too, can live our lives in the same
way Jesus did. Throughout the day I ask the Lord to
show me what He is doing, so that I may do likewise.
It is beginning to happen! Recently two friends of
mine, David and Kathie Walters, said to our congregation that Jesus only did *three* things. He only did
what He saw His Father doing. He only said what
He heard His Father saying. And, He only went
where His Father told Him to go. I have made that
my goal as well.

Does that last statement sound arrogant? Let me assure you that I am fully mindful that I cannot do this in my own strength. But the really "good" news is that I was *never* meant to live in my own strength. God has made a way for you and me to live as Jesus did, with a life and power not our own.

We in the evangelical church tend to major on the work of the cross. Indeed, the cross is key and absolutely essential. Without Jesus' sacrifice there we would still be without hope. No cross, no salvation, no forgiveness, no restored fellowship with God, no nothing! However, that is not all that God did for us. The other part of the story is that Jesus did not stay on the cross. The cross is only an instrument of death. When Jesus died, its purpose was fulfilled. We err if we try to make it do more. The cross is the entrance, the door to eternal life with God. But, my new life comes from a different source. Yes, the cross is our entrance, but our life is in the power of the resurrection.

"Why do you seek the living One among the dead? He is not here, but He has risen."[5]

"Because I live, you will live also..."[6]

Father did not intend to leave us to our own devices. He is much smarter than that! If man was not capable of living in unbroken fellowship with Him *before* the cross, then forgiveness for sin would not be the only requirement to ensure an unbroken relationship after the cross. Otherwise, man would have to continually run back and forth to the cross to see that fellowship restored, again and again... it is a wearisome cycle.

That is what much of the church is taught to do. I was. That is just what I did for years and years. God has a *better* way. Hallelujah!

Every one of us who is Born Again will readily confess that we have been indwelt by the Holy Spirit. If you're like me, the words flow very freely, almost glibly, off the tongue. What I didn't understand is by confessing this I was *agreeing* that the very God of the universe now dwells inside me! I had no idea how big and revolutionary this concept is, but God was and is determined to teach us.

Why would God want to live in and through me? What is His plan?

He redeemed me so that He could fill me with Himself, so that just as He lived through the life of His Son Jesus, He might now also live in and through me. Not only do I really <u>live</u> because of the resurrection, I live <u>through</u> the life of the Resurrected One! "It is no longer I who live, but Christ who lives in me."[7]

Seems pretty simple, doesn't it? I gave mental assent to it for years. But, what has changed for me on this leg of the journey is to comprehend that *He really means it!*

How do I know? He says so. Look again at John 5:19. "Truly, truly I say to you the Son can do nothing of Himself..." That word "nothing" in Greek is and means—"nothing," "not even one". What Jesus is saying here, is that as a man, He could not do even one thing in His own strength. All His miraculous works and words, through the whole of His life, were possible exclusively, by living through the supernatural Life of His Father. Does that seem hard to believe? Let me ask you, would He who is the Truth lie?

Why did He choose to live that way? Two reasons come to mind. One, as the Son of Man, Jesus experienced all our human limitations and did not try to live a life pleasing to the Father without divine help. This should encourage us greatly, because that same divine help is available to us. The resurrection makes available to us the incarnational life of the Son of God. We can be as dependent on His supernatural life in and through us as He was on His Father.

Not only *can* we, we are called *to be* that dependent. "I am the vine, you are the branches; he who abides in Me and I in him, he bears much fruit, for apart from Me you can do nothing."[8]

Guess what? The word "nothing" in this verse is the same one Jesus uses of Himself in John 5:19. If we can grasp it, we are called to be as dependent on His life as He was on His Father's. He really means it when He says, "Apart from Me you can do nothing." But how can this be? The man Jesus had a unique relationship with God the Father. Can He expect us mere mortals to live the same way? Yes! He requires that we live as He did if we are going to bear fruit for the Kingdom. He has made the way for us to live in that same power. It all has to do with what I have come to believe was the ultimate goal of His mission on planet Earth.

1. Colossians 1:27
2. Strong's Hebrew and Greek Dictionaries G3466
3. Hebrews 12:2
4. John 5:19
5. Luke 24:5-6
6. John 14:19
7. Galatians 2:20
8. John 15:5

Study Questions

"The Mystery"

1. In this chapter, we read that Jesus became the Way for us to come back into alignment with God's plan and the Example to model how we could live out that plan.

    - How did Jesus demonstrate these two realities?

    - Look up Galatians 2:20. How does this chapter correlate with this scripture?

Chapter Five

The Incarnation—God in Man!

Why the incarnation? Why did the Son clothe Himself with human flesh?

"For what the law could not do, weak as it was through the flesh, God did: sending His own Son in the likeness of sinful flesh and as an offering for sin, He condemned sin in the flesh."[1]

This is the first reason that comes to mind. Jesus came in the flesh, to live the sinless life, and then to die for our sin. God's holy justice demanded payment for sin. The Scriptures tell us the "wages of sin is death",[2] and that without the shedding of blood there can be no forgiveness.[3] Jesus, "who knew no sin, became sin on our behalf, that we might be become the righteousness of God in Him".[4] This was absolutely essential and we have been saved from the wrath of God and made His children instead![5] Praise the Lord!

But was Jesus only on a "rescue mission"? Much of our evangelical thinking would leave us with that impression. Jesus came to deliver us from sin, save us from hell, and take us to heaven. As glorious as these truths are, I believe that they are not the whole of it. As we have already seen by Jesus' own words, there was more, even while He was on earth.

"He who has seen Me has seen the Father..."[6]

I suggest that Jesus came *to show us the Father*. The incarnation of the Son was to demonstrate to us a powerful truth. When you look at humanity inhabited by divinity, you see the Divine, or should. For us that means when people look at us they should see Jesus.

I knew of a man who had a vision from the Lord. In this vision he saw a goblet, or so it seemed. It was hard to distinguish, because it was encrusted with all kinds of debris. Then, right before his eyes, the debris began to fall off, revealing a pure, crystal wine goblet. However, the goblet was nearly invisible because of the dazzling beauty of the wine it held. The Lord then spoke and told the man that *he* was that goblet! The Lord was going to work in his life to remove the debris so that the wine, which was the life of Jesus, would shine through so brilliantly that when people looked at the goblet they would only see the wine—Jesus! When people ask, "What does Jesus look like?" We want to be able to say with confidence, "He looks like me." How could we ever make that assertion without Him being in us!

"Do you not believe that I am in the Father, and the Father is in Me? The words that I say to you I do not speak on My own initiative, the Father abiding in Me does His works."[7]

Jesus robed himself with humanity to show us how to live in Him. We are to live as deliberately dependent on Him as He was on His Father. He really meant it when He said that he could do nothing of Himself.[8]

How about the incarnation and us?

"I will not leave you as orphans; I will come to you. After a little while the world will no longer see

Me, but you will see Me; because I live, you will live also. In that day you will know that I am in My Father, and you in Me, and I in you."[9]

Jesus spoke these words on the night He was betrayed, before the agony of cross, in order to point His disciples and us *beyond* the cross. He directs us to two truths: One, the resurrection life, both for Him and for us. Two, the incarnation of the Son *into* the children of the Father. Just a few moments later, He would speak of that union as necessary for bearing Kingdom fruit.[10] Would Jesus have spent so much time sharing these thoughts in His last hours that He would be with His disciples if they were only figurative, or spiritual, language? I think not. He meant them as *literally* as He said them. I am convinced that He reserved His most important and intimate truths for last. We would do well to meditate on them and heed them. The Incarnation is for us today. We are called to live by the Life of Another.

Now as soon as we acknowledge the call to live by the Life of Another, we are in trouble. To live by the life of Jesus within me requires something that I am not comfortable with. It means that I need to continually yield to the power of that life. This is where my "Practical Atheism" really flourished. I confessed that Jesus was in my heart, but I did not act at all as though that was a living reality. I thought, no, really believed, that somehow it was up to me to become like Him. Imitation became my goal and quest. But, is that His?

Imitation or Incarnation? There is a classic Christian book by Thomas a` Kempis, entitled *The Imitation of Christ*. Written in the 15th century, the thoughts it sets forth have guided much of the church's approach to Christian life ever since. We all talk about becoming more "Christ-like". Haven't we all said, or heard others talk about how they "want to be more like Jesus"? If only they, we could be more *like* Him... But, is God looking for us to imitate Jesus?

The whole Old Testament is a tragic account of what happens when man tries to follow God's template, the Law, and become more like God, or holy, in his own strength. If people tried and failed for 4,000 years, what makes us think that we can do any better? Yet, that is exactly what we try and do! We thank Jesus and our Father for salvation. We appreciate the cross. We even "cling" to it. But in all our efforts, we keep coming up short of His glory and likeness. Could it be that Father, in His mercy, has provided a better way? It's "Christ in you, the hope of glory."[11]

That 'hope of glory' is not just about future glory. It speaks to the reality of here and now. In His high priestly prayer in John 17, Jesus said that the glory His Father had given to Him, He had in turn given to His disciples, and through them, to us.[12] There is a glory that the Lord wants us to walk in right now. That's how people will *see* Him *in* us. "When Christ, who is our life, is revealed, then you also will be revealed with Him in glory."[13]

You see, our Father knows, that even with the provision of the cross, we are still incapable of living a life that would please Him. The cross was never meant to "fix up" the old man. The cross came so that the "old man" would be crucified.[14] His provision for us is the Life of the only One who ever could please Him.[15] It is the life of Jesus within us that conforms us to His image.[16] This is really "good news"! Father didn't stop at the cross, nor is He just waiting for heaven. He desires to give Life to His people so the whole earth may see His Son in and through them. God is freeing us from fruitless striving and frustration. I don't want to *try* to be "like" Him anymore. I want to yield to the Life within and let Him shine!

---

1. Romans 8:3
2. Romans 6:23
3. Hebrews 9:22
4. 2 Corinthians 5:21
5. Romans 5:9-10, 1 John 3:1-2
6. John 14:9
7. John 14:10
8. John 5:19
9. John 14:19-20
10. John 15
11. Colossians 1:27
12. John 17:20-23
13. Colossians 3:4
14. Romans 6:6
15. Galatians 2:20, 2 Timothy 2:11
16. 2 Corinthians 3:18

Study Questions

"The Incarnation: God in Man"

1. The Son clothed Himself with human flesh for two reasons. What are they?

   Romans 8:3

   John 14:9

2. What two truths did Jesus reveal to His disciples on the night He was betrayed, to point them and us to life beyond the cross? (John 14:19-20)

3. What is the challenge to accepting the call to living by the life of Another?

4. When people see "humanity inhabited by Divinity", they should see _____.

Chapter Six

What does this Life look like?

One of the beauties of the Word of God is that it will always confirm truth in more than one place. We have seen that in regard to Jesus' words in the Gospels. Now let's look at some other New Testament scriptures to see what they have to tell us about living by the Life of Another. Now that my eyes are opened, I am amazed at how many references there are to the reality and power of the Life within. Let's look at a few of them.

"For He rescued us from the domain of darkness, and transferred us to the Kingdom of His beloved Son."[1]

We are now citizens of a New Kingdom. The patterns that dictated our lives in the kingdom of darkness will not work in this one. Praise the Lord! The way we lived, before we became a part of the Son's Kingdom, must change if we are to truly enjoy all its blessings. The King of this Kingdom has established a very clear pattern for His subjects to follow. He demonstrated it when He lived on earth[2] and has decreed it to be the way of life and fruitfulness for all His subjects. Abide in Him, He in us— "Apart from Me you can do nothing" He really means it![3]

"For the love of Christ controls us, having concluded this, that one died for all, therefore all died; and He died for all, so they that live might no longer live for themselves, but for Him who died and rose again on their behalf."[4]

In the kingdom of darkness to which we formerly belonged, the mantras were "Every man for himself!" "Me first!" "Mine, Mine, Mine..." In this new Kingdom, we live *for* Another. We live for our King, so we must live as He shows and directs.

"I have been crucified with Christ; and it is no longer I who live, but Christ lives in me; and the life I live now in the flesh I live by faith in the Son of God, who loved me and gave Himself up for me."[5]

Not only do we live for the King, the King lives *in* us! This truth alone has tremendously freed me and simplified my life and understanding of what the Lord is looking for. Living "by faith in the Son of God" is just that—yielding to His life within. How many weights have fallen away as I have begun to do that!

"...The mystery which has been hidden from the past ages and generations, but has now been manifested to His saints, to whom God willed make to know what is the riches of the glory of this mystery among the gentiles, which is Christ in you, the hope of glory."[6]

He is in us! This is the passage that God used to open my eyes. It happened for me in a remarkable and very public way.

In August of 2002, a team of eight—five Americans, two Kenyans and a Ugandan who pastors in Nairobi, Kenya—traveled to Kampala, Uganda for a several days of special meetings, which our Ugandan pastor friend from Nairobi, James Wesonga, had arranged for us. We had just come from taking part in two weeks of tent meetings in Kenya, and our Kenyan hosts, Jeremiah and Beth Pallangyo, were traveling with us to Kampala. Because of the intense schedule of the previous two weeks, I had not prepared anything new to preach in Uganda, assuming I would draw on the same messages that I had just used. I felt the Lord stirring something in me through those messages as well through the words I had been hearing from others during the crusade, but I had nothing new to give. While on our way to the first meeting at which I was scheduled to speak in Kampala, I became acutely and uncomfortably aware that the Lord was not going to allow me to draw water from the well I used in Kenya. At first, I was seized with a sense of a panic. "What am I going to do now?!" I thought nervously. As the van we were traveling in forced its way through the noontime Kampala traffic, the Holy Spirit dropped a single verse into my spirit— Colossians 1:27. Quickly I opened my Bible to see what the verse said, it was not a particularly familiar passage at that time. "To whom God willed to make known what is the riches of the glory of this mystery among the Gentiles, which is Christ in you the hope of glory." The words did not mean a whole lot to me when I read them. I remember shooting up an urgent prayer, "Lord, what do You want me to do with this?" Here I was the guest preacher, on my way to a gathering of people I had never met who were expecting to hear a word from the Lord, and all I had was one verse. And *no idea* what to do with it! I began to console myself by thinking, "Well this is a lunch hour prayer meeting, maybe there will only be few folks there. Maybe the Lord just wants me to give a greeting and use this verse in it somehow."

Boy was I wrong! You see we were on our way to *the daily* "Lunch Hour Prayer Meeting" at The Lord's Trumpet Ministries, a dynamic little church right in the middle of downtown Kampala. The Lord's Trumpet had been the site of a community—wide 24/7 house of prayer for nearly nine years at the point of our visit. (It is still going strong in 2005). The "Lunch Hour Prayer Meeting" was just one of the "shifts" in this incredible furnace of prayer. It is attended daily by hundreds of Ugandan Christians. Yes, I said hundreds! They spend their lunch hours seeking the Lord on behalf of their nation, the nations of the world, and anything the Lord burdens them for. They also are keenly tuned to God's heart for Israel. When we got there and got settled my wife, Susi, noticed a hand-made poster on the wall calling for prayer for the peace of Jerusalem. Later on when she had opportunity to ask about it she was told that the first watch of every day is for the nation of Israel and the Jewish people.

These people are serious worshippers and prayer warriors too! Before we cleared the threshold of the building we heard the "sound of many waters", as several hundred Ugandan brothers and sisters lifted their voices to the throne of God in praise and intercession. The presence of the Lord in that place nearly knocked us off our feet. I share that, because I believe the Lord used that supernaturally charged atmosphere to release something in me.

We were swept up into powerful intercession against demonically driven political unrest in the north of Uganda. After that a young lady from Britain who had been visiting and working in the outskirts of Kampala gave a greeting and testimony to God's wonders. Then it was my turn. I was sweaty from the intensity of the prayer and the midday heat. I still only had that one verse, and no sense of where to go with it. I had no idea that the Lord Jesus was going to use this very set of circumstances to both humble and promote this preacher from North Chili, NY. After the host's introduction, I stood up cleared my throat and did my best to give a friendly greeting. As I stared at my bible, the Lord told me to look back a couple of verses in Colossians chapter one. I did. I read to myself the verses (24-29), looked at the sea of faces and opened my mouth to speak. Scales suddenly began to fall from my eyes and my understanding. Truth, I had read many times before grabbed me in that moment. Revelation began to flow and I experienced a level of anointing on my mind and words that I had not known before. Even now, as I write this account, tears of wonder and gratefulness are flowing. Jesus was doing what Paul prayed in Ephesians 1:17-18—opening my understanding, the "eyes of my heart" were being enlightened. He was speaking *to* me and *through* me at the same time! For the next two and a half days the flow of revelation and anointing continued, unabated. I preached six or seven more services each time without notes, each time by on the spot revelation from the Holy Spirit, and each time, with a steadily deeper understanding of Christ in me, the hope of glory.

In those few days, my life was irrevocably changed. The flow of revelation that began in Kampala continues to this day. The revelation of Christ in me has changed every aspect of who I am and how I live my life, hence my urgency to write this book. Truth this life changing *must* be shared. Perhaps there are some people reading this who think they know, even believe they understand this concept (like I did). Yet God wants to open their eyes as He has mine. Could that be you?

One final note on this account: Before traveling to Uganda, I had asked the Lord for a spiritual impartation to bring back with me. Through my reading and viewing the "Transformations II" video, I knew some of the history of suffering the church in that land had experienced and also what the Lord had been doing in their midst. In my request for an impartation, I thought I was asking for more of the Spirit and passion for intercession for my own nation and region. I had no idea that He was going to give me a whole new life message!

And yet, I realize that "Christ in me" is not actually a totally new life message at all. The Lord has been patiently, persistently trying to get my attention for years. From my earliest days in the Kingdom He has been speaking to me through various means about the Life within, I just never got it until recently. Here is one example. In the mid-1970's, the Lord gave me a life scripture. It came inscribed on a plaque given to my wife and me by a young friend who was visiting us from Northern Ireland. On the plaque was simply written Ephesians 6:10: "Be strong in the Lord and in the strength of His might." The moment I took that plaque in my hands, I knew that the Lord was speaking those words to me; this verse was meant to be a life scripture for me. Since that time, I have endeavored, with varying degrees of success, to keep that truth before me. I even have used it as a computer screen password, and just got EPH 610 "specialty" license plates for my van. But it is only by the revelation of *living by the Life of Another* that I understand *how* Father has provided for me to be "strong in the Lord". It is "In the strength of His might". But I now know that might is within me, not just outside.

That's why the pattern, showing how to live by the life of Another (John 5:19, 30) is so important. Jesus lived in and by the strength of the Father's might. That might within sustained Him on earth for 33 years. That might within enabled Him to endure the cross, despising the shame. That might also raised Him from the dead. That same might and strength are available to us as well. "How much of it?" you may ask. All of it! We are designed to be filled with all the fullness of God (Eph. 3:19). We, the church, are the fullness of Him who fills all in all (Eph. 1:23). The greatness of the power that raised Christ from the dead is "Toward us who believe" (Eph. 1:19-23). Now that's more good news!

If we really grasp this in our hearts and minds (by revelation) our lives will become greatly simplified. As a practicing, "card carrying", practical atheist, I confessed the power of the cross to save me but, by my perpetual effort to still be accepted by what I do, I virtually denied the power of the Lord to keep me, strengthen me, form me. Now I am no longer striving by own effort and "good" behavior to gain access to His good graces and presence. If I understand the truth that God Himself is really living in me, and that His desire and design is to live through me—then I have all the power of the universe on my "side". Let's explore the way this affects the central issue that every committed follower of Jesus wants to see eliminated in his/her life the most i.e.—Sin. Before the cross, the Bible tells me that my sin had made a separation between

God and me.[7] How many soul winners, in the course of their sharing about salvation, have drawn on restaurant napkins the illustration of the chasm of sin, which can only be bridged by the cross of Christ! This is certainly true. Sin did stand in the way. I could not approach the Holy God because of it. But what is my situation now? Am I still on the outside? Do I still have a barrier of sin that keeps me from God? Do I keep bouncing back and forth from one side of that chasm to the other? How can I be "outside", or separated from Someone Who lives in me?

With Christ in me, it is now *Jesus and me* against my sin. Rather than a barrier to fellowship, I now have an ally in the fight! What a load that should lift from our shoulders! We struggle with many things, but battles fall away when we realize the very God of the Universe is living in us and through us. What chance do temptation and sin have in the face of that knowledge? The devil uses the fear of sin to keep us focused on it and unsettles us in our standing with the Lord. That need be *no more*!

Of course there is a part for us to play. His Life can either be bottled up or released by us. He has limited Himself to our choice and obedience since He formed Adam in the garden. "Obey My voice, and I will be your God, and you shall be My people; and you will walk in all the way which I command you, that it may be well with you"[8] is still true—but now that "voice" is not carved in stone, it is within our hearts. He has written His word on our hearts. He speaks to us by the still small voice of His Spirit within our hearts. But the choice of obedience and release is ours.

1. Colossians 1:13
2. John 5:19,30
3. John. 15:4-5
4. 2 Corinthians 5:14-15
5. Galatians 2:20
6. Colossians 1: 26-27
7. Isaiah 59:2
8. Jeremiah 7:23

Study Questions

"What Does this Life Look Like?"

1. Colossians 1:27 is the scripture the Lord used to open the author's eyes to the living reality of Christ in us. In the space below write out Colossians 1:27 and Galatians 2:20. Re-write them, inserting YOUR NAME for "you" and "I".

Colossians 1:27: _____

_____

Galatians 2:20: _____

_____

Ask the Holy Spirit to breathe fresh life into you through these words.

2. Before receiving salvation, the sin issue went like this: me, my sin, the cross. Now with Christ **in** me, how has that has changed?

Chapter Seven

Which Covenant Now?

I am about to launch into what may well be the most controversial part of this writing. I encourage you, the reader to proceed with me, keeping an open mind and heart. One of the biggest challenges throughout history, in regard to God's progressive revelation of truth to the church, is that the new always challenges the old. The Reformers challenged the Catholic Church. The Pentecostals challenged the Evangelicals. It has always been so. Even Jesus affirmed this principle in the parable of the new vs. old wineskins. I am convinced that what we are talking about in this book is both a revelation of truth being restored to the church and a new wineskin. Some will find it uncomfortable, confrontational, and perhaps even offensive. God is the Lord of all Truth. Only He can bring revelation to any of us. May the Lord give you all that He has for you as we move deeper.

A number of months ago, perhaps even a year or so, the atmosphere in our Sunday morning worship service was pierced by a powerful prophetic word. The Lord's message was short, to the point, and almost startling. "I, the Lord, am going to deliver this church from the Old Testament!" Now before you react prematurely, let me tell you that mine was the voice. This is what I believe the Lord was saying: His intent was not, and is not, to literally deliver us from believing the Old Testament. The Old Testament is as much the Word of God as the New Testament. What I understood Him to mean is that He was going to be delivering us from *thinking* and *acting* as though we are still living under that Old Covenant.

Even though virtually every Believer would say "Amen, Brother!" to that statement, I have come to see that the church draws much of its theology, practice, and music regarding our relationship with God from concepts that are no longer applicable to New Testament saints. We look to the Psalms and many other portions of the Old Testament at what were once totally accurate words for man's relationship to God. We take those same words and concepts and try to bring them into the New Covenant. This is a problem because many of these "truths" have been fulfilled in Jesus and are <u>no longer</u> true of who we are in Him. Let me give you a few examples of the contrasts:

In Christ

- We are called saints, not just "sinners saved by grace"[1] We are no longer to live with an "outer court mentality" seeing ourselves on the outside, still needing atonement. I will cover this truth more thoroughly later in this chapter. It is one of the striking and pervasive characteristics of "practical atheism".
- We no longer have a fallen nature—"heart" desperately wicked and sick.[2]
- We no longer walk in conditional and temporary forgiveness and righteousness, because

we are not under the law of the Old Testament but the Law of the Spirit of Life in Christ Jesus.[3]

The Bible calls us a people filled with "all the fullness of God".[4] How could these former things still be true of us? The truth is they are not. Yet we continue to cling to them.

How we even approach the Lord speaks volumes about which paradigm we really live in. Remember my term "Practical Atheism and the difference between theoretical and operational beliefs? For years we have sung the words of the Psalms: "Enter His gates with thanksgiving and enter His courts with praise."[5] Even Paul exhorts us to make our request with thanksgiving.[6] We do well to follow the principle. However, there is much in contemporary Christianity that points us to worship from the days of the Tabernacle and Temple. In its time, it was God's provision. But rather than realize this system was passing away, totally fulfilled in Christ Jesus, we tend to want to return there and start "entering" again and again. There must be something, which keeps us from receiving the fullness of what God has done. Let's look at this in more depth.

Which court are you in? Where do you see yourself spiritually? Take a moment and think about that. Are you in the outer court? Inner court? *Holy place*? Are you in the Holy Place, or Holy of Holies?

What I am referring to is that under the Old Covenant, man approached God in steps or stages. First there was the outer court of the Temple. The outer court was basically a "spectators" area. Any of the Hebrew people could come here provided they were "ceremonially" clean, according to the Law of Moses and others that were added over time by Rabbis. It was the outer court where the sacrifices were brought to be slaughtered.

In Solomon's temple, the inner court is where the sacrifices were offered on the brazen altar to atone for sin, etc.[7] One had to pass through the outer court and into the inner court in order to offer his sacrifice. That was as far as all but the priests, could go.

The Holy Place was the first chamber of the temple. Here the golden lamp stands were tended to with sacred oil and the flame kept burning, and sweet smelling incense went up before the veil which separated the Holy Place and the Holy of Holies. The innermost sanctuary of the temple was the Holy of Holies. Here rested the Ark of the Covenant, with its golden mercy seat. The very presence of God dwelt between the Cherubim that were over the Ark.[8] The Holy of Holies was off limits to all but the High Priest. Even he could only enter, fearfully, once a year on the Day of Atonement.[9] God set the order of the temple very specifically and strictly. A failure to comply could result in death. There was soberness, rightly so, as God was teaching His people about His holiness and righteousness under the Old Covenant.

Jesus is our High Priest before God. He has satisfied, once for all time the holy demands of God's righteousness for all who call upon His name. He has passed through the outer court, offered Himself up on our behalf in the inner court, and has torn down the veil separating the Holy Place from the Holy of Holies. He has made the way through His own blood, for us to come boldly, all the way into the Holy of Holies.[10] We are called to dwell there in the presence of God. There are many New Testament Scriptures that attest to these things.[11]

If these things be so then why do we still act as if we live in the outer court? Why do we seem to spend so much of our time trying to once again earn our way into the inner court? Why do we often act as though the sacrifice of Jesus was not enough? I have taken note of late as to how we pray, and very often even sing. "Take me past the outer courts... past the brazen altar... into the Holy Place... I want to see you face to face." Has Jesus not already taken us there? Why do we ask Him take us somewhere we already are!

There is much to be garnered from the Old Testament. It is Holy Scripture, and "True", profitable for encouragement, teaching etc. But, God does not now deal with the New Testament saints by Old Testament principles and procedures.

"Outer court" living causes us to be sin focused, because in reality a primary focus of the Old Testament was sin. God had given Israel the Law. The Law was not an end in itself. Rather, it was a means to an end. The end of the Law is that man could not live by the Law.[12] He needed the Grace of God that could only be realized in the Lord Jesus. We read in Galatians that "The Law was a tutor to lead us to Christ."[13] For the believer in Jesus Christ, the purpose of the emphasis on sin in the Old Testament is to show us what we were like, would be like, apart from Him. But, in Him they are no longer true of us. This is so important to grasp. When we draw inaccurate or inappropriate conclusions about our standing with God from the Old Covenant, we rob ourselves of living in the joy and freedom of who we are now in Christ. As it says in 2 Corinthians,

"You are a new creation; old things have passed away; *all* things have become new!"[14]

The focus of the New Testament is not sin. It is Jesus and the revelation of the Father. Through His born again family, the church, the fullness of Him who fills all in all, He wants to reveal Himself and His Father to the whole of mankind.

1.I realize that this idea of "sinners saved by grace" is a concept that has been accepted as fact in the church for many, many years. But does New Testament Scripture support that idea? Yes, if we talk about being saved *from* sin. [Ephesians 2:1-9]. No where in the New Testament are we admonished to continue to call or view ourselves as sinners. Throughout Acts and the epistles followers of Jesus are referred to as saints. [e.g. Romans 1:7, 1 Corinthians 1:2, 2 Corinthians 1:1, Ephesians 1:1, Philippians 1:1, Colossians 1:2]. Paul does refer to himself in one place as a sinner [1 Timothy 1:15]. However, I believe the context supports the idea that he was talking in that instance from a historical and not present tense perspective. He certainly never refers to those he is writing to as other than saints. Do saints still sin? Of course they do. But because they may still struggle with sin in some measure does not make them any longer sinners by nature or appellation.

2. Jeremiah 17:9 says, "The heart is more deceitful than all else and is desperately sick; who can understand it." I say, "Amen. That *was* true of me too, before I became a new creature in Christ Jesus. *Now*, as a follower of Jesus, things are different; 2 Corinthians 5:17 tells me, "Therefore if any man be in Christ, he is a new creature: old things are passed away; behold, *all* things are become new." (KJV italics added) I am a new creature, and I have a new nature. If you know Jesus as Lord, you do too.

3.Romans 8:1-4, Hebrews 9:11-14, Hebrews 10:4, Ephesians 1:7, Ephesians 2:4, Colossians 2:13-14

4.Ephesians 3:19, Ephesians 1:22-23

5.Psalms 100:4

6.Philippians 4:6

7.Leviticus chapters 4-6

8. Chronicles chapters 3-5

9. Leviticus 16:2, 11-14

10. Hebrews 10:19-20

11. John 14:18-20, John 14:27, Galatians 2:20, Hebrews 4:16

12. Romans 8:2-4, Galatians 3:19-24

13. Galatians 3:24

14. 2 Corinthians 5:17

Study Questions

"Which Covenant Now?"

1. In the light of this chapter, where do you see yourself?

   - Are you struggling to live by the law of the Old Covenant?

   - Are you still outside the New Covenant, because you have not yet received the gift of Life through Jesus Christ?

   - Are you a New Testament saint still trying to live an Old Testament lifestyle?

   - Are you a New Testament saint learning to enjoy the freedom of the New Covenant?

2. How does "Outer Court" living cause us to remain sin focused?

Chapter Eight

The Presence Powered Life

In this day God is raising up a people through whom He will extend His Kingdom in all the earth: the Church that will manifest "the fullness of Him who fills all in all".[1] This will require a paradigm shift of astronomical significance. A famous Asian church leader, on his first visit to the States, is reported to have remarked after observing the American church, "It is amazing what they have accomplished without the Holy Spirit." I don't believe he was saying the Holy Spirit is totally absent from the American church. Rather, I think it was a comment directed at our proclivity to take things into our own hands. Even if that observation was slightly accurate (and we know better, don't we?), then just think how much more could be accomplished if all of the church were operating totally under the power of the Life within. I have chosen to call that the "Presence Powered Life".

Pastor Rick Warren of Saddleback Church in Lake Forest, California has written an excellent book entitled, "The Purpose Driven Life".[2] The Lord has been using Rick's book in a powerful way. My use of the term "Presence Powered Life" is not meant to detract from his work in any way. We must know the purpose for which the Lord has called us. The Presence Powered Life speaks to the "how" of fulfilling that purpose. My thesis is that the risen Lord Jesus desires to accomplish that fulfillment by living His life through each one of us just as the Father did through Him 2000 years ago. The fullness of His resurrection life in His Body, the church, is a force that the world has yet to see, but will— soon!

So what does this paradigm shift look like and how do we get there? I believe the shift for the church is from its sole focus on the cross to the power of the resurrection. For 500 + years the church's emphasis has been on the cross and securing eternal life, i.e., escaping hell and, secondarily in our thinking (though primary in God's) escaping the just wrath of an Almighty God. This has put the major focus on what God has done for us through the crucifixion—which is true and wonderful. This primary truth was the power behind the Reformation. The Church has been living off its richness for five centuries, and we will never exhaust the glory of the work of Christ at Calvary.

That firmly stated, it has produced some "side effects", if you will, that God is in the processing of changing. Focusing on one aspect of what the Lord has done *for* us causes us to be short-sighted and self-centered. Our faith has often been fixated on the benefits and blessings. All too often, the result is, if I am enjoying the benefits at the moment, then God is good. On the other hand, if my benefit and blessing quotient dips below a certain level there goes God's rating as well. We have become "Christian Consumers" with faith and commitment all too often tied to God's perceived faithfulness to meet and match our expectations. The epitome of that kind of thinking believes that the next event on God's clock is that He will come and rescue us (rapture us) from all our trouble. We just have to hang in there until then, the "great escape".

But what if God's plan isn't rescue but invasion? What if God's plan is to do what He said, to make all of His Son's enemies His footstool through His victorious church?[3] What if God's plan is to reveal His glory in and through His church, so that the knowledge of the glory of the Lord will cover the earth as the waters cover the sea?[4] What if the "hope of glory" in us, mentioned in Colossians 1:27, is for this life and not merely the next? In Colossians 3:3-4 we read, "For you have died and your life is hidden with Christ in God. When Christ, who is our life, is revealed, then you also will be revealed with Him in glory." Remember as well that Jesus gave His disciples glory while He was still on earth, and that glory has been given to us also.[5] Is the "glory" spoken of in all these verses only for the future life? I don't think so. After all, why would we need to be revealed with Him in glory there? Firstly, everyone in heaven will be in the same "glory" condition. And, secondly, all eyes are going to be riveted on His beauty, not ours. I believe that Father has determined to make all His Son's enemies His footstool. He is going to do that by revealing the glory of the Son through His victorious church, the "fullness of Him who fills all in all".[6] In the process the whole earth is going to be covered with the knowledge of the glory of the Lord and we too will be seen in His glory! Through His Life within us, we have been given the awesome privilege of carrying His glory to the nations!

If these things be true, if what He is giving us in His life and glory are to be revealed this side of heaven, this will require some radical adjustments in:

☐ Theology: The King and His Kingdom within; the King living His life through us before a watching world. "All of creation is waiting for you in me."[7]

☐ Expectations: The Kingdom coming forth in victory and the extension of the King's reign throughout the earth through His Body in the nations.

☐ Practice: If the King is within me and I am in Him, then everywhere I go, He goes! I take the Kingdom with me. How should that influence my actions? How should my actions influence those around me? I want my entire community to see Jesus, to know His love and power. That will happen as I allow Him to live His life through me. Yielding is the key, not trying harder.

This paradigm will release great confidence and authority in the saints. Signs and wonders will flow as His people learn to walk in the reality of carrying His presence all the time. (Cf. the effect of Peter's shadow in Acts 5). If I know the King is in me, I can more readily believe to hear His voice, and believe also for words and actions of divine origin and authority.

- Words of knowledge and wisdom on the job
- Discernment for daily needs and problems
- Healing and creative miracles
- Signs and wonders
- Raising the dead
- Enduring faith in the face of opposition and persecution

- Best of all, a closeness of relationship that is beyond anything I have known before!

The church's most challenging and glorious days are ahead!

'There is a living Spirit of the living God, which will flow through the soul of a man just as it flowed through the soul of Jesus." John G. Lake[8]

1. Ephesians 1:23
2. The Purpose Driven Life, by Rick Warren; Zondervan Publishing copyright 2002
3. Psalm 110:1-3, Hebrews 10:13, Ephesians 1:22-23
4. Isaiah 11:9, Habakkuk 2:14
5. John 17:22
6. Ephesians 1:23
7. Suzi Wills "All of Creation" Eaglestar Productions Romans 8:19
8. John G. Lake The Complete Collection of His Life Teachings, Compiled by Roberts Liardon, Albury Publishing 1999 p.222

Study Questions

"The Presence Powered Life"

1. "What if God's plan isn't rescue, but invasion?"
   Is this a new thought for you?

2. In order for us to fulfill our part in this invasion,
   we may need to make radical adjustments in our
   theology, expectations, and practice. Re-read
   that portion of the chapter. Ask the Holy Spirit to
   lead you in answering the following questions:

   ▪ What areas of my believing/thinking/living
      do I need to adjust?

   ▪ Am I ready and willing to do so?

Chapter Nine

How does this supernatural Life work here and now?

How is this "Presence Powered Life" released? How can I live in it daily? What does it look like?

I am glad you asked! Perhaps the most concise way to describe what we are referring to when we use the phrase, "Presence Powered Life", is to simply state that as Christians we live by the life of Another.[1] How do we come into it? The reality is that by grace we are already there! God has made full provision from before the foundation of the world.[2] The incarnation has already taken place, both in eternity and in history. When Jesus breathed on His disciples in the upper room and said to them, "Receive the Holy Spirit", that was it! He was breathing His own life into them, just as He had breathed "the breath of life" into Adam. In Adam's case it was physical life, with the *potential* for the incarnation. Remember, incarnation has always been God's plan. Since Jesus died and rose again, that "breath" has been the entrance of His very Presence into everyone who believes on Him for salvation. It has already been done, once for all His children. Notice that I said "everyone" and "all His children". He is no respecter of persons, age or gender. This is not a doctrinal or denominational thing. This is spiritual reality. The more open we are to the activity of the Holy Spirit and the supernatural realm, the more consciously we will be able to experience this reality. Doesn't that make you want to say, "Lord, open my eyes and my heart to Your Presence within!"? He is waiting to do just that!

"Faith comes by hearing and hearing by the word of God."[3] "Faith comes from 'hearkening' (hearing and heeding) the word of God", is what the literal Greek says in Romans 10:17. Hearkening to the Word brings revelation to our hearts, and that, in turn, releases faith. Faith is necessary not just for believing, but for acting. James tells us, "Faith without works is dead".[4] Any statement of truth is merely words on the page until it is acted upon. The "Presence Powered Life" is a life of action. Just look at the words. You can't stay unengaged in the Presence of the Lord. And, power is only there to be released. Jesus has indwelt us, because He wants to do stuff we read about in the Book—and more!! The tragedy of the church is that through our ignorance, unbelief, and selfishness, we have kept the very life of the Son of God shut up within these "earthen vessels"! Let's begin to change that right now by asking the Holy Spirit to help us "hearken" to His words.

Galatians 2:20 "I have been crucified with Christ; and it is no longer I who live, but Christ lives in me; and the life which I now live in the flesh I live by faith in the Son of God, who loved me and gave Himself up for me."

There are actually two ways the Greek word "*en*" can be translated. The NASB (above) translates it "in"—"I live by faith *in* the Son of God." The KJV translates the same word as "of" I live by the faith *of* the Son of God". Both have significance for us. We live *in* the Son, and by the power *of* the Son. We live in Him and by Him and for Him.

John 5:19 Therefore Jesus answered and was saying to them, "Truly, truly, I say to you, the Son can do nothing of Himself, unless it is something He sees the Father doing; for whatever the Father does, these things the Son also does in like manner.

As we live in the Son and by His power, we live as Jesus did on earth.
- I do what I see Him doing. I see in His word, in the circumstances around me, and by asking Him to open the eyes of my spirit that I might see the unseen, supernatural realm[5]
- I listen to the still small voice within[6]

When we slow down and yield to this truth it is amazing how much easier our lives will/can become. Jesus did not make this pronouncement or live His life by this example to make *our* lives more complex. No, it's the opposite. Yielding, letting the Lord live through me and direct my steps, takes all the weight of responsibility for pleasing God off my scrawny shoulders and puts it on the only One who can truly do it. As with anything we learn and grow into, this walk starts with small steps. It's in the small things that the patterns of life are formed and matured. Jesus wants to equip us through obedience in the small things. We have spent so much of our lives thinking we are in control it takes time to adjust—shift gears. But we *are* shifting to a higher gear! You could drive all the way to the store and back using only your car's first gear. It is physically possible, but hard on the engine, not very productive, and denies you the power your engine was built to deliver. That is a pretty apt description of my life as a "Practical Atheist". There was a good deal of revving up the engine, spinning the wheels, much, much expended effort, but agonizingly slow progress. I am so thankful to the Lord that He has designed His Kingdom to function on such a more powerful, productive, peaceful level.

So, how do we make the shift?
1. Recognize there is a higher gear!
2. Ask Jesus daily to shift us—My experience began with—and continues with—an at least daily declaration that He is in me and that I am in Him, according to His Word.[7] This creates sensitive ground in my mind and heart that the Holy Spirit can continue to cultivate. This also makes me more prone to actively and consciously turn to His life within me and yield to Him.

- For peace in turmoil
- For strength in weakness and tiredness
- For healing and health
- Wisdom—I have the mind of Christ[8]
- For all the issues and details of life
- For the joy of His fellowship!

I am finding that awareness by itself is making a profound difference in how I view my relationship with Him, myself, and my surroundings. That awareness of His Presence is releasing faith and confidence. Where I go the King goes, and He wants to extend and demonstrate His Kingdom through me, wherever we go.

The Presence filled Life:

It all flows from His Presence in me. Life functions and flows through this awareness of His life within. And the more aware I am, the more I see it happening. Our understanding is catching up with His reality. The temptation is to think that it is up to us to control this, to hold on to the life within. That is to fall into the same old trap—trying to maintain control ourselves will actually frustrate us and hinder His life flow in and through us.

Our part is but to yield. The more consciously we surrender, the easier this becomes. I find myself calling Jesus to live through me with greater ease and frequency throughout the day. He delights to do this. "Apart from Me you can do nothing."[9] The truth brings strength and freedom!

Scripture teaches us that life comes out of death.[10] So, too, in this Presence filled realm. There is a death. For some, initially at least there is a "cross" to bear. The real death/cross is to our compulsion to "have to". To live by the life of Another requires us to surrender control. That can be both scary and humbling. But Jesus is more than a helpful resource for getting through life. He *is* my life!

The ability to live the Presence Powered Life ultimately boils down to this. How literally do we believe the Word of God? I'm going to close this section by restating some of the passages through which the Lord has brought revelation to my own heart. I invite you, the reader, to pause after each one and ask the Holy Spirit to bring fresh discoveries to you as well.

Colossians 1:27 "To whom God willed to make known what is the riches of the glory of this mystery among the Gentiles, which is Christ in you, the hope of glory.

Philippians 1:21 "For to me, to live is Christ and to die is gain."

John 15:4-5 "Abide in Me, and I in you. As the branch cannot bear fruit of itself unless it abides in the vine, so neither can you unless you abide in Me. "I am the vine, you are the branches; he who abides in Me and I in him, he bears much fruit, for apart from Me you can do nothing."

John 14:23 "Jesus answered and said to him, 'If anyone loves Me, he will keep My word; and My Father will love him, and We will come to him and make Our abode with him.'"

Ephesians 3:14-19 "For this reason I bow my knees before the Father, from whom every family in heaven and on earth derives its name, that He would grant you, according to the riches of His glory, to be strengthened with power through His Spirit in the inner man, so that Christ may dwell in your hearts through faith; and that you, being rooted and grounded in love, may be able to comprehend with all the saints what is the breadth and length and height and depth and to know the love of Christ which surpasses knowledge, that you may be filled up to all the fullness of God."

Galatians 2:20 "I have been crucified with Christ; and it is no longer I who live, but Christ lives in me; and the life which I now live in the flesh I live by faith in the Son of God, who loved me and gave Himself up for me."

"How actively does He live in me?"

John 14:19-20 "After a little while the world will no longer see Me, but you will see Me; because I live, you will live also. In that day you will know that I am in My Father, and you in Me, and I in you."

Colossians 3:3-4 "For you have died and your life is hidden with Christ in God When Christ, who is our life, is revealed, then you also will be revealed with Him in glory."

Ephesians 3:20-21 "Now to Him who is able to do far more abundantly beyond all that we ask or think, according to the power that works within us, to Him be the glory in the church and in Christ Jesus to all generations forever and ever. Amen."

---

1. Galatians 2:20, Colossians 1:27
2. Ibid.
3. Romans 10:17
4. James 2:17
5. 2 Corinthians 4:18
6. John 16:13-14
7. John 14:20, John 15:4-5, John 17:20-23
8. 1 Corinthians 2:16, Colossians 2:3
9. John 15:5
10.Romans 6:8

Study Questions

"How Does the Supernatural Life Work Here and Now?"

1. Write a concise definition of the "Presence Powered Life"?

2. In "living by the life of Another", what are our part(s)?_____

Chapter Ten

The Matter of Distrust

Many people do not know the love of God because they do not trust the God who loves them. What is true in human relations is also true in the relationship between the human and the Divine. Unless I trust you, I cannot receive love from you no matter how much you love me. Unless I trust you, you cannot teach me truth. This has always been a struggle for men and women who earnestly want to walk with God, as J. Hudson Taylor testifies in his book "Union and Communion with Christ":

"Could there be a sadder proof of the extent of the fall of man than the deep-seated distrust of our loving Lord and Master which makes us hesitate to give ourselves entirely to Him, which fears that He might require something beyond our powers, *(remember He is the power within—author's comment)* or call for something that we should find hard to give or to do?"[1]

This was the root of my being a practicing "Practical Atheist" for so many years. I did not realize that I distrusted God. I would have insisted vehemently up and down that I did. I had laid my life down in His service and been through deep trials. Many years ago, a prophet declared over me that God saw me as a Joseph. God confirmed His word. I can honestly say that my life has in many ways closely resembled Joseph's. Yet, because of my distrust, the very things, which were meant to be instruments to reveal more of His love for me, instead became impediments to the very Life He had for me.

But God was determined to bring breakthrough! The upheaval began three and a half years ago as I undertook a study of His extravagant love in order to prepare a devotional for our congregation. That study of the scriptures rocked me to the core and revolutionized my understanding of spiritual life. The renewing of our minds has much more to do with discovering who Jesus really is and how much we can/must trust Him than it does with sin issues. The latter is a pre-occupation of the Practical Atheist. I was still trying to get somewhere He has already brought me! You see, distrust of Him springs from ignorance of Him.

What I have subsequently discovered is that trust, yieldedness, surrender, and rest in His love bring Him pleasure. Yes, pleasure! We must never lose sight of the fact that the Lord desires and finds pleasure in us. (Cf. Song of Solomon) We have the incredible privilege of bringing joy to the Creator! "And for Thy pleasure they are created."[2] In this union and communion, Jesus meets our deepest desire for knowing Him and finds, His satisfaction in revealing Himself to yielded hearts.

---

1. "Union and Communion with Christ", J. Hudson Taylor,
   Bethany House Publishers p.20
2. Revelation 4:11 KJV

Study Questions

"The Matter of Distrust"

1. "Many people do not know the Love of God, because they do not trust the God who loves them." Do you agree or disagree?

2. Do you agree with the author's assertion that our yieldedness to the Life within brings the Lord pleasure? Why? / Why not?

Chapter Eleven

The Greater Works

"Truly, truly, I say to you, he who believes in Me, the works that I do shall he do also; and greater works than these shall he do; because I go to the Father." John 14:12

Let's return for a moment to the idea of the "purpose driven life"—here is truly a purpose to live for! To do the works that Jesus did while He was on earth, and even greater works! Wow! Is that pride? No, He proclaims it right here in this verse; this was a promise from Jesus and His Father. Our problem is not pride, but fear and unbelief. But, God is awakening faith in His Body the like of which we have not seen perhaps since the 1st century. God's children are actually beginning to say, "I can do that." "The knowledge of the Glory of the Lord is going to cover the earth as the waters cover the sea."[1] How? Through God's children, that's how. Remember, as we go forth in the earth, Jesus goes forth. "...Because as He is, so also are we in this world."[2]

Where Jesus goes, His glory goes. All of Jesus' works were done to glorify His Father and to attest to who He was. So, too, when *we* do His works, they glorify the Father and attest to who Jesus is. God is beginning the greatest move in history. More people are going to come into the Kingdom in our lifetime than ever before. He is already doing amazing miracles in diverse places on the earth. He has put a hunger in us to see the same in our region. (He is not going to leave us out!) Yes, Lord, renew them in our day.[3]

Jesus is looking for a people who are so yielded to His Extravagant Life that He will have the freedom to do whatever He chooses, whenever He chooses, to whomever He chooses. Father had that kind of love and liberty in the Son. He is looking for it in us. Are you ready for that kind of life? Well, here it is.

---

1. Habakkuk 2:14
2. John 4:17
3. Habakkuk 3:2

Study Questions

"The Greater Works"

1. What does Jesus' term, "the greater works" mean to you?

2. Spend some time thinking about how those "greater works" would affect your world.

3. Are you ready to say, "Yes, Jesus, I am willing to yield to Your life within me. I want to live by the Life of Another, in the power of Your resurrection. I am ready for the greater works." If you are why don't you tell Him so now.

4. Congratulations! You are now embarked on learning how to live by the Life of Another! You will never regret it, or be the same!

Appendix 1

Possession?

What is demon possession in the unbeliever? It is a spiritual reality. Through sin, or trauma of some sort an opening is made in person's soul which gives the devil an opportunity to come in take control of an element of that individual's behavior and or personality. We often talk of someone in that condition as having yielded himself or herself to demonic control. How is it possible for such a thing to happen? We know that the devil can not originate anything. He can only try to pervert, pollute, and mar Gods' design.[1] Furthermore, the devil is the "father of lies."[2] Whatever he says or does is a lie. But, in order for there to be a lie, there must also be truth. If demon possession is a lie, then what is the truth? Is it a perversion of what God has intended for His children through His Spirit? If we can believe in demonic control of a person, can we imagine Holy Spirit control?[3]

In chapter 6, verse 16 of the book of Romans we read, "Do you not know that when you present yourselves to someone as slaves for obedience, you are slaves of the one whom you obey, either of sin resulting in death, or of obedience resulting in righteousness?" We are slaves/servants whichever way we slice it. There is no neutral territory. We will be living by, or under the influence of another. I would much rather living by the life of the Lord Jesus than under the influence of anything else. How about you?

The human soul was never created to be empty—to be uninhabited, "uncontrolled". How else could the demonic take up residence in a person? At the end of a deliverance prayer session, I have often heard those ministering, asking the Holy Spirit to fill that place vacated by the evil spirits. We need to believe that God wants to "control" the life by the grace of Holy Spirit as much as the devil did before. There is a huge difference, however. The devil cannot give us life. But God wants to fill us with His! He has created us with just this in mind. The Christian walk is meant to be a process of growing in our understanding of and yielding to His life within us.

"Lord, I want to be possessed by you. I want to be filled with all your fullness. I want people to see You when they look at me. Amen"

What might that look like?

"Out of your belly will flow rivers of living water."[4] The Life flows from the inside out. When I interact with my surroundings there is to be an impartation of the Life within. Impartation is Jesus in me, giving something to you. He activates an aspect of His life in you that Father wants to use. For example:

- Jesus expressing various of His ministries through us—His supernatural Life and Gifts in every aspect of our world.
- Businessman—Jesus' Kingship, wisdom, character
- Housewife, Mom—Jesus' nurturing ministry
- Fill in the blank—whoever you are, Jesus is whatever you need to demonstrate His life in the world.

---

1. John 10:10
2. John 8:44
3. 2 Corinthians 5:14
4. John 7:37

Appendix 2

Reflect or Radiate?

Are we to reflect God's glory and nature, or radiate it? Is it to be an external or internal reality for us? These are very important questions. If we reflect, then we must be sure that we are always in just the right position to catch the glory in order to reflect it adequately. It also means there could be obstructions that obscure both our view and the glory's transmission, (though certainly not from the Lord's side of the equation). This reflection would require great diligence on our part, a continual monitoring of our state of fitness as reflectors, and our right positioning, A few degrees one way or the other and the reflection will be skewed. This type of thinking lines up with what we have often been taught over the years: We are to Jesus as the moon is to the Sun. As the moon possesses no light of its own, but merely reflects the light of the sun, so we, possessing no light of our own, are to reflect the light radiating from Jesus. Heard that before?

There is no question Jesus radiates light. Hebrews 1:3 says, He "is the radiance of His Glory..." In Jesus dwells the fullness of the Godhead in bodily form.[1] Every aspect of the Father is fully revealed in and through the Son. But what about us? Does the analogy of the sun and the moon hold up to the scrutiny of the Scriptures? First of all, does the Bible say anywhere that we are to be "reflectors"? A word search through "Strong's Concordance" will reveal that the words "reflect" or "reflectors" *never* appear *even once* in the whole of the book. That begs the question, "How can we be called to do something that Scripture does not clearly indicate?" Let's look further to find out exactly what it does contain for us? If we are not "reflectors", then what are we? We know that the radiance of Jesus is given to enlighten the darkness[2] and that He has ordained us to be the vessels through which that happens.[3] So, how does the radiance of Jesus get released?

By His own words, Jesus is the "light of the world."[4] But, in the Scripture Jesus calls us the light of the world also.[5] Jesus said, "As My Father has sent Me, so I send you."[6] How did the Father send Him? He sent Him onto planet earth to be the light of the world, to show forth His glory to mankind. Jesus came so that all men might see Father God. He sends us now with the same assignment. Peter tells us that we have been called that "we might show forth the glory of Him Who called us out of darkness into His marvelous light."[7]

We "show forth" His light by radiating the same light that He Himself is and has. We do not reflect something from the outside. No, rather it comes from within, specifically from the Life of Jesus resident in each of His born again children.

Why is this distinction so important? Today the Lord is releasing in the earth an understanding of His ways through His people that will release a greater demonstration of Who He is than any other time since perhaps the 1st century. In fact, the revelation will be greater because God always does greater than what He has done before. He never goes backward. Glory to glory!

---

1. Colossians 2:9
2. John 1:4
3. Matthew 5:14
4. John 8:12
5. Matthew 5:14-16
6. John 20:21
7. 1 Peter 2:9-10

Epilogue

Much has happened since that fateful day in Kampala in 2002. The revelation of "Christ in you" has continued to grow and mature within and around me. Growth is God's job. Learning to respond to Him is ours. Believe it or not, learning to slow down and *yield* to the Life within is often the biggest challenge for us. It has been such a joy to watch others "get it", here at home and over seas. In fact, some of the most dramatic breakthroughs have taken place in Africa.

In May of 2004, I was invited to return to Kampala. I brought with me, Tim Brumbaugh, a young man from our congregation who had begun to understand and walk the revelation of the Presence Powered Life. Tim and I were invited to return to Kampala and minister on this theme at the church of Apostle E. Steven Kabunga. Apostle Kabunga had been my host for the trip in 2002. He had remarked after that initial visit how much his own life and ministry had been changed by the message. He wanted us to come and minister it to his whole church. In the course of a week of daily meetings, we watched as the Lord took these dear saints from having no understanding of the Power within them, to the place where they not only embraced Jesus' life, they wanted let Him loose on their streets! During the last two days, we sent them out by twos for short forays into the neighborhoods around their church. The testimonies of salvations, deliverances, prophetic ministry, and healings they came back bubbling over with were right out of the book of Acts! One team of two young men actually saw an

entire medical clinic emptied as they experienced
Jesus healing through them! To my knowledge this
church continues to grow in the revelation of Christ
in them and the daily release of His life and power.

We have also witnessed some life-transforming
results in Kenya. Here are some brief testimonies I
have received from brothers and sisters with whom we
shared this message.

"It was a lovely and blessed year 2004 when
Apostle Carl Jenks shared a message of mystery....He
spoke about Jesus Christ being the mystery and also
the hope and glory in us. God is also restoring mysteries
and revelation back to the church of Jesus Christ. God
has kept riches, revelation for our generation. He
continued to speak to the church that if we understand
that Christ in us is the hope of glory we shall start to
move in power...He concluded by saying that we are
king bearers and Christ carriers...my life has never
been the same again."

Sarah Wairimu
New Hope for All Nations Church
Naivasha, Kenya

"How I have benefited from Pastor Carl
Jenks's ministry. It was back in the year 2002 when
I first met him, and my heart was ministered to
through his message full of incredible revelations...He spoke not just to change believers
emotionally, but with a profound truth spoken to the
inner person—enlightening the eyes to clearly
comprehend the mystery of Christ...I have personally greatly broadened my understanding through
this message. Since I have received this great revelation, I have entered new levels spiritually and

physically, also in my area of ministry the anointing came and things changed tremendously."

J.M. Njenga
New Hope for All Nations Church
Naivasha, Kenya

"This message changed my life completely. [Pastor Carl] told us a mystery according to Colossians 1:25-27 which reminds us that HE did not send His Son only to forgive our sins, but He sent Him to live in us too. When I discovered this, I changed some of my singing, eg. 'Jesus, do not pass me by when You are visiting others.' This means my worship life and singing changed, because I understood that Jesus lives in me; He does not come and go...Now I know God wants to use me, and I have seen Him helping me in my personal life and ministry...Through this teaching, I have realized I am a carrier of the glory of God; I am infectious, contagious, and dangerous!...This was an explosion in my heart, and this has been such a blessing to my life as a whole and my worship ministry."

Ruth Muthoni Njenga
New Hope for All Nations Church
Naivasha, Kenya

These are just examples of how God is releasing this message, "The Presence Powered Life", throughout the earth. Weekly here at home, more and more people are starting to awaken to the revelation and the reality of Christ in them. My prayer is that you too will begin that journey and experience the joy and adventure of supernatural living Jesus has for you.

I would welcome hearing from you as your journey unfolds.

Bibliography

Fromke, DeVern F. The Ultimate Intention. Cloverdale: Sure Foundation, 1963.

Jenks, Carl B. Extravagant Love. Rochester: New Hope Community Church, 2002.

Kempis, Thomas á. Imitation of Christ. New York: Grosset & Dunlap, 1978.

Lake, John G. John G. Lake: The Complete Collection of His Life Teachings. Compiled by Roberts Liardon. Tulsa: Albury, 1999.

Lawrence, Brother. The Practice of the Presence of God. New Kensington: Whitaker House, 1982.

Taylor, Hudson J. Union and Communion with Christ. Minneapolis: Bethany House, 1971.

Thrall, Bill, Bruce McNicol, and Ken McElrath. The Ascent of a Leader. San Francisco: Jossey-Bass, 1999.

Warren, Rick. The Purpose Driven Life. Grand Rapids: Zondervan, 2002.

Author Contact Information

Carl B. Jenks
c/o New Hope Community Church
3355 Union Street
PO Box 279
North Chili, NY 14514

E:mail: cjenks@newhopecom.org

Visit our website at www.newhopecom.org

Other Resources

From Carl Jenks:

Month-long devotionals:
Extravagant Love
Walking in His Extravagant Love
His Extravagant Life

From New Hope Community Church

Keep Drawing Me – a CD of original prophetic praise and worship

Printed in the United States
61969LVS00002B/1-99

9 781599 510026